D0993354

THE
WEIRDEST
NATIVITY

Andrew Sach
& Jonathan Gemmell

a division of 10 of those.com

Copyright © 2019 by Andrew Sach and Jonathan Gemmell

First published in Great Britain in 2019

British Library Cataloguing in Publication Data
A record for this book is available from the British Library

ISBN: 978-1-912373-88-8

Designed and typeset by Pete Barnsley (CreativeHoot.com)
Cover illustration by Chris Iliff Illustration (chrisiliff.co.uk)

Printed in Denmark by Nørhaven

10Publishing, a division of 10ofthose.com
Unit C, Tomlinson Road, Leyland, PR25 2DY, England

Email: info@10ofthose.com
Website: www.10ofthose.com

1 3 5 7 10 8 6 4 2

DEDICATION

To Jack Wilde, Andrew's godson,
whose brother once dressed as a
dragon for a weird nativity;
and to persucted Christians
around the world

THE WEIRDEST NATIVITY

The school nativity was a bit different this year. Of course there were the usual last-minute costumes: the tea-towel-and-dressing-gown shepherds; the Burger-King-crown wise men; the awkward Joseph, trying to keep a safe distance from a Mary who was taking her betrothal far too seriously. Everyone was impressed at the Sinclair twins' donkey costume and it was no surprise that Ella, not one to hide from the limelight, came dressed as a star with a six-foot span.

But why was Harry dressed as a dragon? Why was there a lamb in the manger? Why, in this health-and-safety-conscious age, were there shards of broken pottery all over the floor?

And what was with the grinning baby holding a crowbar?

This really was the weirdest nativity!

Disturbed parents were quick to point the finger at Mr Latimer, the new Religious Studies teacher, but he seemed unfazed by their criticisms. A week later, at his disciplinary tribunal, he calmly picked up a Bible, turned to the back and began to read aloud of a dragon, a crowbar, smashed pottery and a lamb. The school governors were dumbfounded. It was the Christmas story as they'd never heard it before, but it turned out that Mr Latimer's nativity was legit after all.

We are more familiar with the Christmas story as recorded by Matthew and Luke. Matthew tells us that Jesus was born of a virgin in the little town of Bethlehem, in fulfilment of surprisingly specific ancient prophecies. He records the visit of Magi from the east, who followed a star to find the newborn King and presented him with gifts of gold, frankincense and myrrh. But he doesn't mention a dragon.

Luke begins his narrative by setting out his methodology as a historian: he interviewed the eyewitnesses to find out exactly what happened. He goes on to describe how the angel Gabriel appeared to Mary, announcing her miraculous pregnancy. Later, angels brought an announcement to shepherds who were watching over their flocks at night:

> *Do not be afraid. I bring you good news that will cause great joy for all the people. Today in the town of David a Saviour has been born to you; he is the Messiah, the Lord.[1]*

Luke is meticulous with historical detail. But curiously he overlooks the big red dragon.

Although John doesn't record the birth of Jesus, the opening chapter of his gospel is often read at Christmas. It speaks of light coming into the world; the Word becoming flesh; 'the glory of the one and only Son, who came from the Father, full of grace and truth'.[2]

At the end of his life, John wrote another book, which is now found at the end of the Bible. Persecution had arisen against the first followers of Jesus, and John was exiled to the Greek island of Patmos. There he received a revelation of

Jesus Christ. It's a frightening vision, full of shocking imagery, describing hidden spiritual realities of the present and the future. Here be dragons!

You may have heard of the four horsemen of the apocalypse, and you almost certainly know that 666 is the number of the beast, but in all likelihood you have come across them in horror movies, stripped of their original meaning. Sadly John's book has also been hijacked by crazies who use it to guess the exact timing of the end of the world – not really his intention at all!

The problem is that neither Hollywood nor the doomsday prophets treat the book of Revelation *as a vision*. When they read of a dragon with seven heads, they imagine something physical, an unexpected member of the reptile family, rendered in realistic 3D thanks to a multimillion-dollar special effects budget. But John is writing down what he saw in a dream, even a nightmare. It's metaphorical, figurative, symbolic. It's the difference between you or I taking a photograph of a woman, and Picasso painting the same woman. In our photograph you can see the size of her nose and the colour of her eyes. Picasso doesn't even care if she *has* a nose! Instead he gives you a powerful impression of her – much more powerful than our photograph in fact. John is doing a Picasso. When he writes of dragons, lambs and crowbars, it's not that he's caught on camera something that Matthew and Luke missed. Rather he's trying to capture the meaning and gravity of it all. He's showing us the same Christmas from a remarkable perspective.

THE DRAGON IN THE MATERNITY WARD

A great sign appeared in heaven: a woman clothed with the sun, with the moon under her feet and a crown of twelve stars on her head. She was pregnant and cried out in pain as she was about to give birth. Then another sign appeared in heaven: an enormous red dragon with seven heads and ten horns and seven crowns on its heads. Its tail swept a third of the stars out of the sky and flung them to the earth. The dragon stood in front of the woman who was about to give birth, so that it might devour her child the moment he was born.[1]

John's vision begins in a maternity ward with a woman about to give birth. No prizes for guessing that the baby is Jesus. But who is the mother? On first reading we might assume that it's the Virgin Mary – she, after all, was the one who gave birth to Jesus. But we need to tune in to John's picture language. Mary was an ordinary teenager from the town of Nazareth in Israel. She presumably wore average first-century, Middle Eastern clothes. But this woman is dressed with the sun, stands on the moon and wears a hat made of twelve stars. That is anything but average!

The number twelve in the Bible frequently refers to the twelve tribes of Israel, the people whose story is told in the Old Testament. Perhaps you've heard of how God rescued them out of slavery in Egypt through a prophet called Moses; that he gave them the Ten Commandments; that he brought them into a Promised Land, flowing with milk and honey; that he gave them a king called David and promised that one of his descendants would reign for ever and ever.

The woman with the twelve-star hat in John's vision is Israel herself: a nation not an individual. When John tells us that the *nation* gives birth to a child, it's his way of saying that the child is part of this bigger Bible story, the climax of more than a thousand years of expectation.

Let's continue working through the cast list. We've identified the woman and her baby. The one character who remains a mystery is the 'enormous red dragon with seven heads and ten horns and seven crowns on its heads'. A few verses later, John will unmask him as 'the devil, or Satan'.[2]

Picture the scene in the hospital: the woman reclined in bed; the midwife trembling in the corner; the dragon poised, ready to devour the child the moment he is born. It's disturbing – not the kind of image you want to see behind one of the doors of your chocolate Advent calendar; not the kind of song Mariah Carey would have dreamt of including on her Christmas album.

And it seems a bit far-fetched. At the mention of the devil, many modern readers switch off. The dragon is someone we would expect to see in a pantomime, but he's surely not a topic of serious discussion for enlightened twenty-first-century minds? Stop. Before you dismiss it all as fanciful nonsense, we invite you to consider a few of the historical facts.

At the time of the first Christmas, Israel was part of the vast Roman Empire. Herod the Great had conquered the region from the Hasmoneans in 37 BC, and was tolerated by the Romans as a puppet king. He is famous for some incredible building projects, notably the Herodium, an impregnable fortress in a hollowed-out mountain. (Sorry Bond villains – Herod got there first.) He was, by any estimate, a megalomaniac.

You probably remember Herod from the famous Christmas story of the wise men and the star:

> *After Jesus was born in Bethlehem in Judea, during the time of King Herod, Magi from the east came to Jerusalem and asked, 'Where is the one who has been born king of the Jews? We saw his star when it rose and have come to worship him.'*
>
> *When King Herod heard this he was disturbed, and all Jerusalem with him.*[3]

He was disturbed because the title 'king of the Jews' was one he had taken for himself. And he was not willing to vacate his throne for some baby:

> Herod called the Magi secretly and found out from them the exact time the star had appeared. He sent them to Bethlehem and said, 'Go and search carefully for the child. As soon as you find him, report to me, so that I too may go and worship him.'[4]

… 'worship' in this case being a synonym for 'brutally kill'. The only reason Herod wanted intel from the Magi was so he knew where to dispatch his death squad. Yet thanks to a divine tip-off, the wise men decided it would be best not to return to Herod but to sneak back home by another route. His murderous plan was thwarted, and in his rage he showed his true colours:

> When Herod realised that he had been outwitted by the Magi, he was furious, and he gave orders to kill all the boys in Bethlehem and its vicinity who were two years old and under, in accordance with the time he had learned

from the Magi. Then what was said through the prophet Jeremiah was fulfilled:

'A voice is heard in Ramah,
*   weeping and great mourning,*
Rachel weeping for her children
*   and refusing to be comforted,*
*   because they are no more.'*[5]

Bruegel the Elder, a sixteenth-century Flemish painter, attempted to portray the scene in his famous 'Massacre of the Innocents' (google it). At first glance, it looks like a Christmas card: leafless trees in silhouette, snow-topped cottages, a street carnival. Then your eye is drawn downwards and you notice a platoon of soldiers with their spears raised. Then in the bottom third of the canvas you see the horror of Herod's orders being carried out – except that the painting, which now hangs in Windsor Castle, was famously 'censored'.[6] However experts have used infrared imaging techniques to recover the grisly original:

... a standing woman grieves over her dead baby lying in the snow (changed to an array

of hams and cheeses); a couple seem to beg a soldier to take their daughter rather than kill their baby son (changed to a goose or swan) … A group of soldiers stab with pikes at a pile of babies (changed to livestock) to ensure that they are all dead; women run off in horror as another Lansquenet stabs a baby (changed to a young boar); a soldier stabs at a baby (changed to a pitcher) cradled by a seated woman.[7]

The biblical account of the slaughter at Bethlehem is absolutely in keeping with what we know about Herod from other historical sources. He was paranoid that his wife Mariamne wanted to poison him, and so had her executed. He prosecuted three of his sons – Alexander, Aristobulus and Antipater – for treason, and they too were executed. The Emperor Augustus reportedly joked that 'I'd rather be Herod's pig than Herod's son'.[8] (Being Jewish, Herod didn't eat pork, so a pig had a greater chance of survival.)

Towards the end of his life, concerned that his citizens might not be sad to see him go (perceptive, that!), Herod hatched a brilliant plan: herd a bunch of famous people into the hippodrome in Jerusalem and 'the moment I expire have them surrounded by the soldiers and massacred; so shall all Judaea and every household weep for me, whether they want to or not.'[9]

It's obvious why John's visionary maternity ward didn't contain a dachshund. Or a dormouse. The historical background demanded that it be a dragon. It had to be terrifying and violent and destructive.

But actually John is not saying that Herod *was* the dragon. John believes in an unseen supernatural power who works behind and through human tyranny, a puppetmaster who pulled the strings of the puppet king and countless other tyrants throughout human history. John believes that evil is real.

Compare the view of Richard Dawkins, the famous atheist:

> *In a universe of electrons and selfish genes, blind physical forces and genetic replication, some people are going to get hurt, other people are going to get lucky, and you won't find*

any rhyme or reason in it, nor any justice. The universe that we observe has precisely the properties we should expect if there is, at bottom, no design, no purpose, no evil, no good, nothing but pitiless indifference.[10]

There is no evil, says Dawkins. It's all just random numbers. Herod murdering children was random numbers. Auschwitz and Belsen were random numbers. The killing fields of Cambodia were random numbers. Kony's child soldiers in Uganda were random numbers. 9/11 was random numbers. Sexual violence is random numbers. Stabbings of teenagers on the streets of London are random numbers. You see, we now have a perspective that's so much more enlightened than the Bible.

Hardly. It's those who deny the existence of the devil who are living in a world of make-believe. In the real world, murder is objectively wrong. In the real world, spiritual forces are at work. In the real world, at the first real Christmas, a dragon was pitted against a newborn.

The only question is, who won?

THE BABE IN
THE CHINA SHOP

She gave birth to a son, a male child, who 'will rule all the nations with an iron sceptre.' And her child was snatched up to God and to his throne. The woman fled into the wilderness to a place prepared for her by God, where she might be taken care of for 1,260 days.[1]

At this point, John's vision speeds up like a time-lapse video: we get thirty-three years in half a sentence. Jesus is born, and the next thing you know he is raised up to God's throne in heaven. If you're at all familiar with the life and ministry of Jesus, you'll know there's quite a lot that gets missed out. John has no time to describe

Jesus' extraordinary miracles – the feeding of the 5,000; walking on water; turning water into wine; healing the lame; giving sight to the blind. He has no time for Jesus' radical teaching – 'Do to others as you would have them do to you';[2] 'Do not judge, or you too will be judged';[3] 'turn … the other cheek'.[4] He skips Judas's betrayal; Peter's threefold denial before the cock crows; Pilate's kangaroo court. He doesn't even pause to tell us of Jesus' death on the cross.

John is in a hurry to get to the final chapter in which the baby wins, the dragon loses and the battle is over almost as soon as it has begun. Given his brevity, the things he *has* chosen to include merit careful attention. The mention of a crowbar, aka 'iron sceptre', is of enormous significance.

About a thousand years before Jesus, King David wrote a coronation hymn. It found its way into Israel's songbook, the book of Psalms, and would have been well known to most of John's readers. Let's treat it as if it were a bulletin for the *News at Ten*:

[Cue opening sequence. Cue Big Ben striking the hour. And roll.]

Why do the nations conspire
    and the peoples plot in vain?
The kings of the earth rise up
    and the rulers band together
    against the LORD and against his
    anointed, saying,
'Let us break their chains
    and throw off their shackles.'⁵

*'News just in from the United Nations. The
Security Council has passed a unanimous
resolution and all 193 member states have
pledged their support. Saudi Arabia and
Iran are shaking hands on it! Donald Trump
and Kim Jong-un are posing yet again for a
photograph. They have all declared war on
… God! The political narrative is clear: they
are portraying the generous, life-giving God as
a despot who has enslaved them. They claim
they would be better off without him, living
without reference to his divine government.
They are screaming for him to be overthrown.'*

The One enthroned in heaven laughs;
    the Lord scoffs at them.

He rebukes them in his anger
   and terrifies them in his wrath, saying,
'I have installed my king
   on Zion, my holy mountain.'[6]

'We now cross live from New York to our own correspondent in God's heavenly throne room – to hear the Almighty's response to this attempted coup. Is there something wrong with the microphone? It seems to be picking up the deep rumblings of … a belly laugh? Yes, God's laughing! He considers the whole thing a colossal joke. Not that he's pleased. He just finds the rebellion pitiful. "Your grasp at power won't work," he says. "I have installed my king."

'We now bring you an exclusive interview, recorded with the newly enthroned Messiah himself. He is about to share with us what Almighty God said to him behind closed doors! Some listeners may find aspects of this material disturbing.'

I will proclaim the Lord's decree:
He said to me, 'You are my son;
   today I have become your father.

Ask me,

> *and I will make the nations your inheritance,*
> *the ends of the earth your possession.*

You will break them with a rod of iron;

> *you will dash them to pieces like pottery.*[7]

'We have here in our Jerusalem studio our Religious Affairs Correspondent, Claudia Chan, to help us understand the key concepts. Claudia, welcome. Can we start with what the Messiah means when he said God became his father. Is it some kind of cosmic adoption process?'

'No, he's talking about the moment he received the crown. The Christian doctrine of the Trinity recognises that Jesus has always been the "Son of God", but that's not what is meant here. The words were also used to describe the kings of Israel. Jesus became "Son of God" in this kingly sense at the moment of his resurrection.[8] It's a royal title.'

'And breaking the nations with a rod of iron? Can you tell us more about that?'

'It's a warning to the rebels. He's got an iron rod. You've got a bone china teapot. Can you seriously imagine going into battle with

the King of the Universe, armed with nothing
but a Royal Doulton tea service?'

'So you're saying they have no hope of
winning this war?'

'Absolutely. Their war on God was based on
a lie in the first place. And to imagine they can
overthrow him is delusional. Give up, guys.
You can't win this.'

[The anchorwoman now turns to camera to
address her audience directly.]

Therefore, you kings, be wise;
    be warned, you rulers of the earth.
Serve the LORD with fear
    and celebrate his rule with trembling.
Kiss his son, or he will be angry
    and your way will lead to your destruction,
for his wrath can flare up in a moment.
    Blessed are all who take refuge in him.[9]

[Cue News at Ten credits.]

Now we are in a position to understand John's
image of a baby with a crowbar. He is the

King of the nations, crowned the 'Son of God' as he rose from the grave. Of course he is still opposed. Many in the world today disbelieve him, or defy him, or dismiss him as irrelevant. Some continue to pedal the fake news that God is a cosmic spoilsport. Some still try to escape his rule. But from God's perspective the rebellion is laughable. It's too late: the King is on the throne. The only sensible response is to kneel before him in worship, for he wields an iron rod.

As the ultimate story of good versus evil, you might think this is a bit lame. It's not a protracted battle, stretched out over several films like a Peter Jackson trilogy. The sides are not evenly matched: Jesus is born and then he wins. The end.

But it turns out it's not the end. We haven't seen the last of the dragon. He has been defeated, but not yet destroyed. The woman, representing the people of God, has fled into the wilderness and has gone into hiding for 1,260 days (more on that later). And the dragon is coming after her …

THROWN OUT OF COURT

Then war broke out in heaven. Michael and his angels
fought against the dragon, and the dragon and his
angels fought back. But he was not strong enough,
and they lost their place in heaven. The great dragon
was hurled down – that ancient snake called the devil,
or Satan, who leads the whole world astray. He was
hurled to the earth, and his angels with him.

Then I heard a loud voice in heaven say:

'Now have come the salvation and the power
  and the kingdom of our God,
  and the authority of his Messiah.
For the accuser of our brothers and sisters,

who accuses them before our God day and night,
has been hurled down.
They triumphed over him …"[1]

In the last chapter, we saw the baby Jesus step into the ring and deliver the knock-out punch to the dragon. Now we see that this cosmic blow, delivered on earth, has repercussions in heaven. Satan and his entourage are 'hurled down' by the hand of the archangel Michael, in his role as God's bouncer.[2]

To appreciate how Jesus won, we need to understand something of the dragon's fighting style. He is called 'Satan', which in Hebrew means 'the accuser'. It's a fitting nickname because that's what he does: he accuses people.

Let's change the metaphor from the boxing ring to the courtroom. Imagine the scene. You are in the dock. The God of heaven is at the judge's bench. He needs to call no witnesses for he has your every thought and word and deed recorded in his books. In steps the counsel for the prosecution. You notice he wears seven wigs, one for each of his heads. They are all slightly askew as they sit awkwardly upon his protruding horns. The dragon is determined to push for a conviction.

When God has heard the case, he will pass the most final of all sentences. The guilty face more than life in prison with the prospect of early parole. They will suffer eternal punishment.

Just as the atheists scoff at the existence of evil, so they are dismissive of the idea of God's judgment. If they are right, and heaven and hell are just fantasies, then a criminal only has to worry about evading justice in this life. The Jimmy Saviles of the world really have died and got away with it; the rampaging gunman whose final act is to turn the gun on himself faces nothing but extinction. For the atheist, the cosmos is justice-less, consequence-less, hope-less.

But Jesus disagreed. He often spoke of judgment, and backed up his claim that death was not the end by emerging alive from the tomb. His resurrection is proof that we must take our eternal destiny seriously.

So back to our courtroom image. Satan rises from his seat, opens the first of a huge stack of lever-arch files and begins to accuse you. He starts with your earliest memory: the time you pulled your sister's hair because she wouldn't let you play with the Fisher Price garage. But then as he moves through your teenage years and into adulthood, you wince as he reads aloud shameful secrets that you thought were long forgotten: malicious thoughts you had, hurtful words you spoke, shameful things you did, compassionate things you failed to do. You don't know where to look. If this were an earthly courtroom, or a challenge by friends in a pub, you might try to face it down. You'd deny it. You'd plead mitigating circumstances. But this is God's courtroom, and you rightly sense this judge already knows that it's all true. Your default excuses – 'There are a lot of people worse than me'; 'I've always tried my best'; 'No one is perfect' – seem rather feeble and, wisely, you don't try them. A guilty verdict is inescapable.

As you are completely undone by Satan's accusations, you desperately fumble around in your memory for some theological loophole. At last you remember the charismatic preacher at

Harry and Meghan's wedding and his repeated refrain, 'God is love'. Colour returns to your face. Your trembling hand is stilled. God is love! He will forgive me!

But it's not as simple as that. God is not a slot machine, where we put in an 'I'm sorry' and out comes an 'I forgive you'. The Bible does say that God is love. But it also insists that he is just. He won't sweep our wrongdoing under a giant heavenly carpet. He despises corrupt earthly courts where victims are denied justice and he would be a hypocrite if he ran heaven the same way.³ No, the Bible assures us, 'The Lord … does not leave the guilty unpunished.'⁴

Hopefully you are beginning to grasp the gravity of the situation you are in.

But we need to stop for a moment, because we are in danger of misreading John's courtroom vision. All we've said above is true – there really is a judgment day awaiting everyone who has ever lived – but John is more focused. When he speaks of 'the accuser of our brothers and sisters', he is thinking specifically of his *Christian* readers. Although they were having a horrible time on earth in the first century, facing all kinds of persecution, *they* had nothing at all to fear from a heavenly perspective. Thanks to the baby with an iron rod, their accuser has been hurled down. He is disbarred from the heavenly court. His case against them will not be heard. These Christians have 'triumphed over him', says John.

You probably want to know how.

THE SILENCE
OF THE LAMB

They triumphed over him by
the blood of the Lamb ...[1]

If you were to take a random sample of the UK
population and ask them who will go to heaven (if
they believe in heaven), most would probably say
'good people'. You don't have to be intelligent, or
beautiful, or talented, or sporty. But the consensus
is that you have to be good. After all God isn't going
to let Hitler or Josef Fritzl in, and he's certainly not
going to turn Mother Teresa away.

'They triumphed over him by being good' –
interestingly that's not what John's vision says at
all. He doesn't think that Christians are less guilty

than anyone else. That's not the reason they escape heavenly charges. Rather he says, 'They triumphed over him by the blood of the Lamb'.

The Lamb is Jesus, and the reference to his blood points to his sacrificial death on the cross. The image would have made immediate sense to John's Jewish readers because just as we celebrate Christmas in December every year with roast turkey, they celebrated the Passover in March or April every year with roast lamb.

Travel back in time with us to around 1,400 years before Jesus. God's people were slaves in Egypt and the Pharaoh at the time – perhaps Ramses II, whose vast statue now dominates Room 4 of the British Museum – made their lives bitter with hard labour. Worse still, in a move that spookily foreshadowed the later actions of Herod, his insecurities led him to order the execution of their male children.

In their anguish the Israelites cried out to God in prayer. God knew that the Pharaoh would not willingly give up his slaves 'unless a mighty hand' compelled him and so God determined to do just that.[2] He sent ten terrible plagues against the dragonish Pharaoh. The water of the Nile was turned to blood; then frogs covered the land, then gnats (think Scotland in August), then flies; then all the livestock died; then everyone was covered with boils; then huge hailstones fell, big enough to smash trees; then locusts devoured the whole harvest; then came a supernatural darkness that lasted three days. But the tenth plague was the worst of all: God announced that at midnight every firstborn son in the country would die. Yet for those who trusted him, there was a way of escape:

Then Moses summoned all the elders of Israel and said to them, 'Go at once and select the animals for your families and slaughter the Passover lamb. Take a bunch of hyssop, dip it into the blood in the basin and put some of the blood on the top and on both sides of the door-frame. None of you shall go out of the door of your house until morning. When the LORD goes through the land to strike down the Egyptians, he will see the blood on the top and sides of the door-frame and will pass over that doorway, and he will not permit the destroyer to enter your houses and strike you down.

'Obey these instructions as a lasting ordinance for you and your descendants. When you enter the land that the Lord will give you as he promised, observe this ceremony. And when your children ask you, "What does this ceremony mean to you?" then tell them, "It is the Passover sacrifice to the Lord, who passed over the houses of the Israelites in Egypt and spared our homes when he struck down the Egyptians."'3

And so, on that fateful night in Egypt, each Israelite family sat down to a meal of roast lamb. Making sure that the lamb's blood they had painted on the door was clearly visible, they nervously tucked their children into bed. Then they waited.

They didn't have to wait long. Soon a cry of terror was heard from the Egyptians as they discovered that the plague had struck. Soon Moses would be called to an emergency summit at the palace. Soon Pharaoh would admit defeat. Soon the Israelite slaves would be liberated!4

But true to God's word, none of the firstborn in lamb's-blood-marked houses were harmed.

Every year thereafter, on the anniversary of the Passover, Jewish families celebrated with a meal of roast lamb. They remembered how God rescued them from the tyranny of Pharaoh by ten plagues. They remembered how God rescued them from the tenth plague by the blood of a lamb.

One year, a Jewish man celebrated the Passover in an upstairs room in Jerusalem with twelve friends. The atmosphere at the table was tense because he had just told those gathered that one of them would betray him. Then, as he passed around the bread and wine, he said something even more uncomfortable: 'this is my body ... This is my blood.'⁵ The man was Jesus. Later that evening, just as he predicted, he was betrayed. The next morning, he was crucified.

Jesus had identified himself with the sacrificial lambs whose blood had marked out the Israelite houses more than a millennium earlier. Because those lambs died, the Israelite firstborn didn't experience the plague. Because Jesus died, Christians will not face God's judgment.

That explains why, just as Jewish families celebrate the Passover, so Christians celebrate the crucifixion of Jesus. They call the anniversary *Good* Friday. They eat a symbolic meal of bread and wine during which they repeat Jesus' words 'this is my body ... This is my blood.' Some wear crosses around their necks. And if you've ever been to church with real Christians, you'll know they love to sing about it!

A few chapters before John describes the weirdest nativity, he has a vision of a throne in heaven, with thunder and lightning flashing from it, surrounded by worshippers both human and angelic. At the centre is 'a Lamb, looking as if it had been slain'.[6] Everyone is falling on their faces before the Lamb, and they sing this song:

> *You are worthy ...*
> *because you were slain,*
> > *and with your blood you purchased for God*
> > *persons from every tribe and language and*
> > *people and nation.*[7]

To say that Jesus 'purchased' these worshippers is to use the language of the slave auction. As the Israelites were slaves in Egypt, so Christians were once slaves to sin. But Jesus paid the price of their freedom with his own blood. His death sets Christians free.

A few chapters later John has another vision:

After this I looked, and there before me was a great multitude that no one could count, from every nation, tribe, people and language, standing before the throne and before the Lamb. They were wearing white robes and were holding palm branches in their hands. And they cried out in a loud voice:

'Salvation belongs to our God,
who sits on the throne,
and to the Lamb.'[8]

To say that Jesus brought 'salvation' to these worshippers is to use the language of rescue. Just as the Israelites were in danger of the plague at midnight, so all of us are in danger of facing God's fierce anger at our sin. But Jesus' death saves those who trust in him.

Then – and this is our favourite bit in the whole of John's vision — someone asks him a question:

'These in white robes – who are they, and where did they come from?'

I answered, 'Sir, you know.'

And he said, 'These are they who have come out of the great tribulation; they have washed their robes and made them white in the blood of the Lamb.'[9]

It's such a crazy image. Imagine it is the morning of your wedding. It takes you ages to get ready, do your hair and the like. You know it will be a long time before you sit down to eat at the wedding reception, what with the service and the photographs and so on, and so before you set off to the church you sit down with your bridesmaids / groomsmen (delete as applicable) for a bacon sandwich. As you bite into it, a dollop of brown sauce squirts out all over your wedding dress / white shirt. Oh no! But then your friends tell you not to worry. You just need to wash it quickly in blood, and it will come out whiter than white.

What? Dipping a wedding dress in blood does not ordinarily result in a white dress! Washing powders are not marketed with blood as a key ingredient. But when the stain on our clothes is not brown sauce but the filth of moral failure, then the blood of Jesus is the one thing that can cleanse us. Though our 'sins are like scarlet,' says the Bible, 'they shall be as white as snow; though they are red as crimson, they shall be like wool.'[10]

Let's return at last to the weirdest nativity. Satan has been hurled down, his case thrown out of heaven's court. Christians are not harmed by his accusations for they have triumphed over him. How? By the blood of the Lamb.

For those who have been *purchased* and *saved* and *cleansed* by Jesus' death on the cross, there can be no condemnation on the day of judgment. It is the only hope of a clear conscience. It is the only hope of vindication in heaven's court.

If only we could have ended the story there. But we've cut John's vision off mid-sentence, and it's about to get ugly.

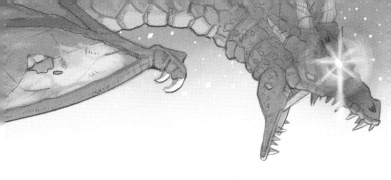

THE STORM
BEFORE THE CALM

They triumphed over him
   by the blood of the Lamb
   and by the word of their testimony;
they did not love their lives so much as to
shrink from death.
Therefore rejoice, you heavens
   and you who dwell in them!
But woe to the earth and the sea,
   because the devil has gone down to you!
He is filled with fury,
   because he knows that his time is short.

When the dragon saw that he had been hurled
to the earth, he pursued the woman who had

given birth to the male child. The woman was given the two wings of a great eagle, so that she might fly to the place prepared for her in the wilderness, where she would be taken care of for a time, times and half a time, out of the snake's reach. Then from his mouth the snake spewed water like a river, to overtake the woman and sweep her away with the torrent. But the earth helped the woman by opening its mouth and swallowing the river that the dragon had spewed out of his mouth. Then the dragon was enraged at the woman and went off to wage war against the rest of her offspring – those who keep God's commands and hold fast their testimony about Jesus.[1]

We've covered quite a few TV genres so far in this little book – horror, news bulletin, boxing, courtroom drama. Now it's time for a Bourne movie, i.e. one sustained, nail-biting chase sequence. Having been kicked out of heaven, Satan rampages against Christians on earth. On the one hand they enjoy divine protection – the woman is taken care of beyond the snake's reach – but on the other hand they experience his constant attacks.

It's something that John's original readers would have been able to identify with. In first-century Turkey, where they lived, Christians were marginalised, maligned and even martyred: 'they did not love their lives so much as to shrink from death.' And things were to get worse. Consider this letter by the Roman Governor Pliny to the Emperor Trajan a few decades later:

> Meantime this is the course I have taken with those who were accused before me as Christians. I asked them whether they were Christians, and if they confessed, I asked them a second and third time with threats of punishment. If they kept to it, I ordered them for execution.[2]

Their experience is not unique. The website www.opendoorsuk.org maintains a watch list of countries where Christians today are at risk of being killed for their faith. In the West, where persecution is currently less extreme, Christians are nonetheless the subject of ridicule at work, or gossip in the neighbourhood, or pitying concern from the family. If the devil is not always breathing fire, believers at least have to endure the stench of his breath.

You've probably worked out by now that our aim in writing this little book is to persuade you to become a Christian. And perhaps you're thinking how strange it is that we should include this chapter. But when Jesus called for disciples, he refused to hide potential hardships in the small print. He was very clear that those who came after him must 'take up their cross', face hatred from the world, and pick a fight with a dragon.[3] If you switch sides to join Jesus, in some ways your life will get more difficult.

So why would you bother? Why is it worth it?

One of the most striking answers to that question comes from a man called Polycarp, who was killed for his faith in the middle of the second century. After threats that he would be thrown to the lions didn't make him flinch, his Roman interrogator said:

'I will have you consumed by fire, since you despise the wild beasts, unless you change

your mind.' But Polycarp said: 'you threaten with a fire that burns only briefly and after just a little while is extinguished, for you are ignorant of the fire of the coming judgment and eternal punishment, which is reserved for the ungodly. But why do you delay? Come, do what you wish.'[4]

Polycarp knew that while he faced the dragon's fire on earth, he would be spared from the fire of God's judgment on the final day. Satan may prevail against him in the Roman court, but in the higher court of heaven he knew his accuser's case had been thrown out. His conscience was now washed clean by the blood of the Lamb, the Jesus who died for him. He knew that the same Jesus was now raised from the dead, seated at the right hand of God in heaven. He knew that the same Jesus was armed with an iron crowbar, ready to defeat all of his enemies. The choice between betraying Christ and being killed was a no-brainer: 'For eighty-six years I have been his servant, and he has done me no wrong. How can I blaspheme my king who saved me?'[5]

Being on the winning side is worth a battle. Eternal security is worth temporary hardship. God's forgiveness is worth human accusation. Gaining Christ is worth losing everything.

If you can cope with a challenge, let's delve briefly into the most enigmatic of all of John's symbols: the period of 'time, times and half a time' (which, if we do the arithmetic, is equivalent to 1 + 2 + ½ = 3½ years or the 1,260 days mentioned earlier).[6] The number has its origin in the prophecy of Daniel, who foresaw that God's people would face a terrible period of persecution.[7] Daniel's predictions were partially fulfilled in 167 BC, when the Seleucid king Antiochus Epiphanes subjected Jerusalem to a three-and-a-half-year reign of terror.[8] But afterwards there was a great victory. Jesus then alluded to the same prophecy when he predicted that Jerusalem would again be besieged and destroyed – as it was by the Romans in 70 AD.[9] But afterwards the church continued to grow.

How does this offer comfort to John's readers? They know that the dragon's attacks are always limited by a divine timetable. They may be gruesome, but they will not be forever. Afterwards, said the prophet Daniel, would come Christ's everlasting kingdom, the final judgment and resurrection of the dead.[10]

It's a rare luxury for sufferers to know that their struggle is finite. If the prisoners in Auschwitz at Christmas 1944 had known that in just over a month they would have been liberated, it would have given them hope. If you knew when starting chemo that it would be only three months until the doctors gave you an 'all-clear', you could cope better with the nausea. Wonderfully Christians know what the enraged dragon himself knows — that 'his time is short'.

The weirdest nativity comes in the twelfth chapter of Revelation, the final book of the Bible. We can't hope to tell you the rest of the story in the few pages we have remaining. But we thought you should know how it all ends:

Then I saw 'a new heaven and a new earth,' for the first heaven and the first earth had passed away, and there was no longer any sea. I saw the Holy City, the new Jerusalem, coming down out of heaven from God, prepared as a bride beautifully dressed for her husband. And I heard a loud voice from the throne saying,

'Look! God's dwelling-place is now among the people, and he will dwell with them. They will be his people, and God himself will be with them and be their God. "He will wipe every tear from their eyes. There will be no more death" or mourning or crying or pain, for the old order of things has passed away.'[11]

For those who change sides to follow Christ, the future is glorious. The devil is eventually destroyed. The world is made new. Tears are gone. We will live in a perfect world forever.

GOD REST YE MERRY GENTLEMEN?

A couple of weeks after the end of term, many parents had forgotten the scandal of the school nativity play. Life moved on. There were turkeys to cook, presents to wrap, in-laws to host, Christmas specials to watch, Christmas number ones to listen to.

Some were just too burned out from work to contemplate cosmic questions of good and evil, just wanting light-hearted fun with the kids. Although they hated the cold, and had no realistic prospects of ever saddling a reindeer, they found themselves humming along to the most trivial of seasonal ditties:

Jingle bells, jingle bells, jingle all the way.
Oh what fun it is to ride in a one-horse open sleigh!

They just kept living life as if the Lamb didn't matter, and as if evil were fantasy, and as if 'I've lived a good life' would be an adequate excuse on the final day. Their thoughts were focused elsewhere: 'Let's get up early tomorrow, darling. Maybe we can grab a bargain in the Boxing Day sales?'

Others were too preoccupied with their own troubles to give further thought to the King who rules the nations. Having gone through a messy breakup, they became irritated by the endless repeats of George Michael on the radio, lamenting what happened when he gave away his heart 'last Christmas'. It didn't occur to them to turn to the King who would never let them down.

Still others had been troubled by the story of the dragon. They knew there was such a thing as evil in the world – in their own lives – and at times it seemed out of control. They hoped to settle their nerves with a generous glass of wine and some soothing classical music. But sitting down to watch *Carols from King's* on BBC 2, they were startled by the words of the traditional 'Coventry Carol':

Lully, lullay, thou little tiny child,
Bye bye, lully, lullay.

Herod the King, in his raging,
Chargèd he hath this day
His men of might in his own sight
All young children to slay.

Lully, lullay, thou little tiny child,
Bye bye, lully, lullay.

Their thoughts returned abruptly to the events of first-century Bethlehem – the Saviour who was born; the tyrant who wanted him dead; the baby; the dragon; the heavenly courtroom; the record of all of our guilt; the Lamb whose sacrifice could wash us clean; the promise of a new heaven and a new earth, with no more death, or mourning, or crying, or pain – and they realised that nothing could be more terrifying or wonderful if it were true.

One of them started to meet a Christian friend once a week to look at part of the Bible together. The weirdest nativity had felt like jumping in at the deep end, so before reading more of John's vision, he wisely decided to cover one of the more straightforward first-century biographies of Jesus: Luke's gospel. The deal was that he would first read a chapter on his own, making scribbles in the margin to indicate things he liked, or disagreed with, or didn't understand. Then he would meet the friend in Costa to go through his annotations.

Another went online to www.christianity explored.org, and discovered there was a course running near where she lived. She found it friendly, informal and unintimidating. Although she had some big questions of her own, for the first few weeks she chose to just sit quietly and listen to what others had to say. Gradually she began to understand more about Jesus.

Still another started to go along to church on Sunday. He decided he wouldn't just go to the one round the corner, but would make an effort to find a church that wouldn't water down the difficult bits of the Bible's message. He wanted the full story – dragons, sin, judgment day, blood sacrifice and all.

A year later, despite protests from family members and taunts from colleagues, a few of these people had begun to follow Christ. They bravely joined the community against whom Satan is most enraged. But they knew in their hearts the wonder of forgiveness, the assurance of victory and the hope of eternity.

And as Christmas came again, they discovered that the words of another well-known Christmas carol were more poignant than they had ever realised:

> *God rest you merry, gentlemen,*
> *Let nothing you dismay,*
> *Remember Christ our Saviour*
> *Was born on Christmas Day*
> *To save us all from Satan's power*
> *When we were gone astray.*
> *O tidings of comfort and joy,*
> *Comfort and joy;*
> *O tidings of comfort and joy.*

ENDNOTES

The Weirdest Nativity

1. Luke 2:10–11

2. John 1:14

The Dragon in the Maternity Ward

1. Revelation 12:1–4

2. Revelation 12:9

3. Matthew 2:1–3

4. Matthew 2:7–8

5. Matthew 2:16–18

6. The changes were made when the painting came into the possession of the Holy Roman Emperor Rudolf II, probably because he

discerned that Bruegel was drawing parallels between Herod's atrocity and the dragonish behaviour of the King of Spain, to whom Rudolf was related.

7. www.rct.uk/collection/405787/massacre-of-the-innocents

8. Macrobius, *Saturnalia* 2:4:11.

9. Josephus, *Jewish War* 1:659–60.

10. Richard Dawkins, *River Out of Eden* (Basic Books, 1995), p. 133.

The Babe in the China Shop

1. Revelation 12:5–6

2. Luke 6:31

3. Matthew 7:1

4. Matthew 5:39

5. Psalm 2:1–3

6. Psalm 2:4–6

7. Psalm 2:7–9

8. The title has its origins in an ancient promise that God had made to King David through the prophet Nathan: '… when your days are over and you rest with your ancestors, I will raise up your offspring to succeed you, your own flesh and blood, and I will establish his kingdom … I will establish the throne of his kingdom for ever. I will be his father, and he shall be my son' (2 Samuel 7:12–14).

   Jesus is 'Son of God' in several different ways. It can refer to him being crowned King at his resurrection (see Acts 13:32–33; Romans 1:4). It can refer to him as the new Israel, in whom all of that nation's hopes would be fulfilled (see Matthew 2:15, comparing Hosea 11:1 and Exodus 4:22). It can refer to his humanity, as a descendant of 'Adam, the Son of God' (Luke 3:38). It can refer to his divinity, as the one and only Son of the Father (see, for example, John 5:19–23; 10:29–30).

9. Psalm 2:10–12

Thrown Out of Court

1. Revelation 12:10–11

2. The biblical prophecy of Daniel explains Michael's involvement in the restraint of Satan before the final judgment day when all of the dead are raised (Daniel 12:1–2).

3. Isaiah 5:22–23

4. Exodus 34:6–7

The Silence of the Lamb

1. Revelation 12:11

2. Exodus 3:19

3. Exodus 12:21–27

4. Exodus 12:29–42

5. Matthew 26:26–28

6. Revelation 5:6

7. Revelation 5:9

8. Revelation 7:9–10

9. Revelation 7:13–14

10. Isaiah 1:18

The Storm Before the Calm

1. Revelation 12:11–17

2. 'Letter from Pliny the Younger to the Emperor Trajan, c. 112 AD', in J. Stevenson (ed.), *A New Eusebius* (SPCK, 1987), p. 18.

3. Mark 8:34; Luke 6:22

4. 'The Martyrdom of Polycarp', in Michael W. Holmes (ed.), *The Apostolic Fathers* (Baker Academic, 2007), pp. 317–19.

5. 'The Martyrdom of Polycarp', p. 317.

6. Elsewhere John refers to the same period as '42 months' (Revelation 11:2), perhaps intending further parallels with the forty-two encampments of the Israelites in the wilderness earlier in their history (Numbers 33:5–49). He then arrives at the figure of 1,260 days by reckoning months of thirty days each (as did most ancient peoples before Julius Caesar changed the calendar).

7. Daniel 7:25; 12:7. (A few verses earlier,

the prophet also namechecks Michael, the angelic bouncer whom we met earlier.)

8. Josephus, *Jewish War*, 1:19 and 5:394; see also 2 Maccabees 5:11–14.

9. Matthew 24:15–21; Luke 21:20–24

10. Daniel 7:26–27; 12:1–2

11. Revelation 21:1–4. This is the beginning of the final section of the book. The very last words are: 'The grace of the Lord Jesus be with God's people. Amen' (22:21).

Andrew Sach and **Jonathan Gemmell** are both members of Grace Church Greenwich and work together at The Proclamation Trust.